Impressionist Masterpieces
from the Musée d'Orsay

Did you know that before the Impressionists created their new style of painting, French artists mainly painted pictures about historical events or made portraits of kings and queens and noblemen? Around the 1870s a number of artists began to try new ways of painting and new subjects, too. Using visible brushstrokes (something not done before) they painted hillsides, boats on the river, towns, and parks, and when they painted people, it was the people they encountered in their daily lives—town merchants, workers in the fields, family members. Both color and light were very important to the Impressionists. They tried to capture the way light appeared in a single moment—on water, on a tree, on a house—and how that changed the way colors appeared. One art critic, who didn't like this new style, dismissed a painting as being just an "impression," and that is how they got their name!

You'll find 22 Impressionist paintings in this coloring book. They are shown as small pictures on the inside front and back covers. When you color in the line drawings, you might want to copy their colors, or you might decide to use your own.

We've left the last page of this book blank so that you can draw and color a picture of your own. How will you capture an impression of your world? Can you use color in new ways?

All works of art are from the collection of the Musée d'Orsay in Paris.

1. Paul Signac (1863–1935), *Women at the Well,* 1892. Oil on canvas, 195 x 131 cm (76¾ x 51⅝ in.). Musée d'Orsay, RF 1979 5.

2. Pierre-Auguste Renoir (1841–1919), *Young Girls at the Piano,* 1892. Oil on canvas, 116 x 90 cm (45⅝ x 35½ in.). Musée d'Orsay, RF 755.

3. Paul Gauguin (1848–1903), *Arearea (Joyousness),* 1892. Oil on canvas, 75 x 94 cm (29½ x 37 in.). Musée d'Orsay, RF 1961 6.

4. Édouard Manet (1832–1883), *The Fifer,* 1866. Oil on canvas, 161 x 97 cm (63⅜ x 38¼ in.). Musée d'Orsay, RF 1992.

5. James Tissot (1836–1902), *The Dreamer,* or *Summer Evening* (detail), c. 1881. Oil on wood, 34.9 x 60.3 cm (13¾ x 23¾ in.). Musée d'Orsay, RF 2254.

6. Henri Rousseau (1844–1910), *The Snake Charmer,* 1907. Oil on canvas, 169 x 189.5 cm (66½ x 74⅝ in.). Musée d'Orsay, RF 1937 7.

7. Pierre-Auguste Renoir (1841–1919), *A Dance in the Country,* 1883. Oil on canvas, 180 x 90 cm (70⅞ x 35½ in.). Musée d'Orsay, RF 1979 64.

8. Vincent van Gogh (1853–1890), *Van Gogh's Bedroom at Arles,* 1889. Oil on canvas, 57.5 x 74 cm (22⅝ x 29⅛ in.). Musée d'Orsay, RF 1959 2.

9. Paul Sérusier (1864–1927), *The Flowery Barrier,* 1889. Oil on canvas, 73 x 60 cm (28¾ x 23⅝ in.). Musée d'Orsay, RF 1980-52.

10. Edgar Degas (1834–1917), *The Dancing Lesson* (detail), 1873–1876. Oil on canvas, 85 x 75 cm (37⅜ x 29½ in.). Musée d'Orsay, RF 1976.

11. Paul Sérusier (1864–1927), *Still Life: The Artist's Studio,* 1891. Oil on canvas, 60 x 73 cm (23½ x 28¾ in.). Musée d'Orsay, RF 1984-11.

12. Berthe Morisot (1841–1895), *The Cradle,* 1872. Oil on canvas, 56 x 46 cm (22 x 18⅛ in.). Musée d'Orsay, RF 2849.

13. Georges Seurat (1859–1891), *Port-en-Bassin, Outer Harbor, High Tide,* 1888. Oil on canvas, 67 x 82 cm (26⅜ x 32¼ in.). Musée d'Orsay, RF 1952-1.

14. Félix Vallotton (1865–1925), *Misia at Her Dressing Table,* 1898. Oil on cardboard, 36 x 29 cm (14⅛ x 11⅜ in.). Musée d'Orsay, RF 2004-1.

15. Edgar Degas (1834–1917), *The Racetrack: Amateur Jockeys Near a Carriage,* 1876–1880. Oil on canvas, 66 x 81 cm (26 x 31⅞ in.). Musée d'Orsay, RF 1980

16. Vincent van Gogh (1853–1890), *Imperial Crown Fritillarias in a Copper Vase,* 1887. Oil on canvas, 73 x 60.5 cm (28¾ x 23⅞ in.). Musée d'Orsay, RF 1989 23.

17. Frédéric Bazille (1841–1870), *Family Reunion* (detail), 1867. Oil on canvas, 152 x 230 cm (59⅞ x 90½ in.). Musée d'Orsay, RF 2749.

18. Théo van Rysselberghe (1862–1926), *Man at the Helm,* 1892. Oil on canvas, 60.2 x 80.3 cm (23¾ x 31⅝ in.). Musée d'Orsay, RF 1976 79.

19. Paul Cézanne (1839–1906), *Kitchen Table (Still Life with Basket),* 1888–1890. Oil on canvas, 65 x 80 cm (25½ x 31½ in.). Musée d'Orsay, RF 2819.

20. Paul Cézanne (1839–1906), *Portrait of Mme. Cézanne,* 1888–1890. Oil on canvas, 47 x 39 cm (18½ x 15⅜ in.). Musée d'Orsay, RF 1991-22.

21. Alfred Sisley (1839–1899), *The Moret Bridge,* 1893. Oil on canvas, 73.5 x 92.5 cm (29 x 36¾ in.). Musée d'Orsay, RF 1972 35.

22. Paul Gauguin (1848–1903), *Breton Peasants,* 1894. Oil on canvas, 66 x 92.5 cm (26 x 36⅜ in.). Musée d'Orsay, RF 1973 17.

Pomegranate Communications, Inc.
Box 808022, Petaluma CA 94975
800 227 1428   www.pomegranate.com

Pomegranate Europe Ltd.
Unit 1, Heathcote Business Centre, Hurlbutt Road
Warwick, Warwickshire CV34 6TD, UK
[+44] 0 1926 430111
sales@pomeurope.co.uk

Photographic copyright for all images:
Photograph © RMN (Musée d'Orsay) / Hervé Lewandowski

© 2010 Fine Arts Museums of San Francisco

Catalog No. CB120

Designed and rendered by Susan Koop

Printed in Korea

19 18 17 16 15 14 13 12 11   10 9 8 7 6

1. Paul Signac, *Women at the Well*

2. Pierre-Auguste Renoir, *Young Girls at the Piano*

3. Paul Gauguin, *Arearea (Joyousness)*

4. Édouard Manet, *The Fifer*

5. James Tissot, *The Dreamer, or Summer Evening* (detail)

6. Henri Rousseau, *The Snake Charmer*

7. Pierre-Auguste Renoir, *A Dance in the Country*

8. Vincent van Gogh, *Van Gogh's Bedroom at Arles*

9. Paul Sérusier, *The Flowery Barrier*

10. Edgar Degas, *The Dancing Lesson* (detail)

11. Paul Sérusier, *Still Life: The Artist's Studio*

12. Berthe Morisot, *The Cradle*

13. Georges Seurat, *Fort-en-Bassin, Outer Harbor, High Tide*

14. Félix Vallotton, *Misia at Her Dressing Table*

15. Edgar Degas, *The Racetrack: Amateur Jockeys Near a Carriage*

16. Vincent van Gogh, *Imperial Crown Fritillarias in a Copper Vase*

17. Frédéric Bazille, *Family Reunion* (detail)

18. Théo van Rysselberghe, *Man at the Helm*

19. Paul Cézanne, *Kitchen Table (Still Life with Basket)*

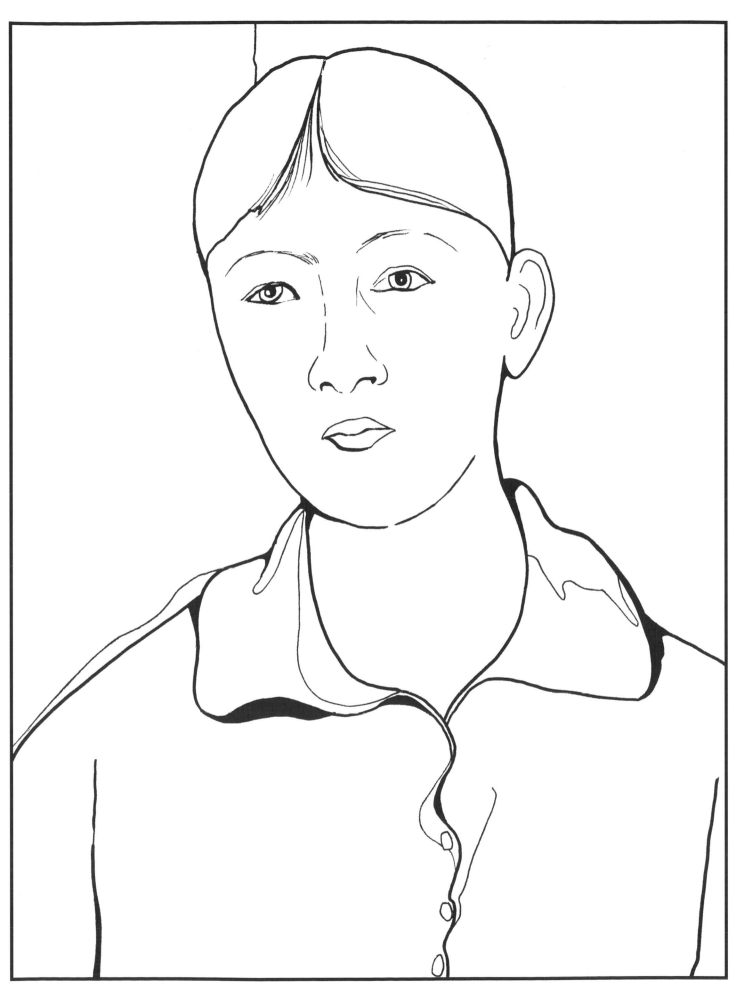

20. Paul Cézanne, *Portrait of Mme. Cézanne*

21. Alfred Sisley, *The Moret Bridge*

22. Paul Gauguin, *Breton Peasants*

Draw and color your own picture here!